Date: 4/25/16

J 970 ROU
Roumanis, Alexis,
North America /

NORTH AMERICA

Alexis Roumanis

LET'S READ
AV²
BY WEIGL™
ADDED VALUE • AUDIO VISUAL

Go to **www.av2books.com**, and enter this book's unique code.

BOOK CODE

A 5 8 3 7 8 4

AV² by Weigl brings you media enhanced books that support active learning.

AV² provides enriched content that supplements and complements this book. Weigl's AV² books strive to create inspired learning and engage young minds in a total learning experience.

Your AV² Media Enhanced books come alive with...

Audio
Listen to sections of the book read aloud.

Video
Watch informative video clips.

Embedded Weblinks
Gain additional information for research.

Try This!
Complete activities and hands-on experiments.

Key Words
Study vocabulary, and complete a matching word activity.

Quizzes
Test your knowledge.

Slide Show
View images and captions, and prepare a presentation.

...and much, much more!

Published by AV² by Weigl
350 5ᵗʰ Avenue, 59ᵗʰ Floor New York, NY 10118
Websites: www.av2books.com   www.weigl.com

Library of Congress Cataloging-in-Publication Data

Roumanis, Alexis.
 North America / Alexis Roumanis.
    pages cm. -- (Exploring continents)
Includes bibliographical references and index.
ISBN 978-1-4896-3042-1 (hard cover : alk. paper) -- ISBN 978-1-4896-3043-8 (soft cover : alk. paper) --
ISBN 978-1-4896-3044-5 (single user ebook) -- ISBN 978-1-4896-3045-2 (multi-user ebook)
1. North America--Juvenile literature. I. Title.
E38.5.R68 2014
970--dc23
                                        2014044128

Printed in the United States of America in Brainerd, Minnesota
1 2 3 4 5 6 7 8 9 0 18 17 16 15 14

122014   Project Coordinator: Jared Siemens
WEP051214   Design: Mandy Christiansen

Weigl acknowledges iStock and Getty Images as the primary image suppliers for this title.

NORTH AMERICA

Contents

Welcome to North America.
It is the third largest continent.

6

This is the shape
of North America.
Europe and Africa lie
to the east of North
America. South America
sits to the south.

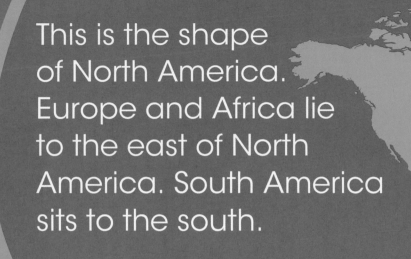

Where Is North America?

Arctic Ocean
Arctic Ocean
NORTH AMERICA
Europe
Asia
Pacific Ocean
Atlantic Ocean
Africa
South America
Indian Ocean
Australia
N
W   E
S
Antarctica

Three oceans touch the
coast of North America.

North America is made up of many different landforms. Deserts, mountains, plains, and rainforests can all be found in North America.

The Great Basin Desert is the largest desert in North America.

Tongass National Forest is the largest forest in the United States.

The Great Lakes is the largest group of fresh water lakes in the world.

The Rocky Mountains stretch about 3,000 miles (4,800 kilometers) across North America.

The Mississippi River is the longest river in North America.

North America is home to some of the world's most unique animals. Many different kinds of animals live there.

The polar bear is the largest kind of bear in the world.

The California condor is the largest flying bird in North America.

North America is home to many different types of plants.

Sugar maple trees make a sweet sap that people can eat.

A bristlecone pine in California is the oldest living tree in the world.

Corn was first grown by people in Mexico.

California redwoods are the largest and tallest trees in the world.

The Venus flytrap can eat small insects and animals.

The United States is one of the oldest countries in North America. It is more than 235 years old. People have lived in North America for thousands of years.

The Blackfoot are one of the first peoples of North America.

Many kinds of people live in North America. Each group of people is special in its own way.

People in Hawai'i greet visitors with flower necklaces called leis.

American Indians often wear feathers for special events.

More than 358 million people live in North America. The country with the most land in North America is Canada.

The city with the most people in North America is Mexico City.

There are many things that can be found only in North America. People come from all over the world to visit this continent.

Old Faithful in Wyoming is a geyser that erupts about every 90 minutes.

More water passes over Niagara Falls than any other waterfall on Earth.

The El Castillo pyramid in Mexico is more than 1,000 years old.

The Grand Canyon in Arizona is about 277 miles (446 kilometers) long.

The White House in Washington, D.C., is more than 200 years old.

North America Quiz

See what you have learned
about the continent
of North America.

What do these pictures tell you
about North America?

23

KEY WORDS

Research has shown that as much as 65 percent of all written material published in English is made up of 300 words. These 300 words cannot be taught using pictures or learned by sounding them out. They must be recognized by sight. This book contains 79 common sight words to help young readers improve their reading fluency and comprehension. This book also teaches young readers several important content words, such as proper nouns. These words are paired with pictures to aid in learning and improve understanding.

Page	Sight Words First Appearance
4	is, it, the, to
7	of, this, three, where
8	all, and, be, can, different, found, great, group, in, made, many, mountains, states, up, water, world
9	about, miles, river
10	animal, land, letter, together
11	home, kind, live, most, some, there
12	a, by, eat, first, make, people, plants, that, tree, was
13	are, small
15	for, have, more, old, one, than, years
16	American, each, its, often, own, way, with
17	from, on, their
19	city, country
20	any, come, Earth, every, only, other, over, things
21	house, long, white

Page	Content Words First Appearance
4	continent, North America
7	Africa, coast, Europe, oceans, shape, South America
8	deserts, forest, lakes, landforms, plains, rainforests, United States
10	bison, Canada geese, pronghorn
11	bird, California condor, polar bear
12	corn, Mexico, pine, sap
13	insects, redwoods, Venus flytrap
15	Blackfoot
16	American Indians, events, feathers, Hawai'i, necklaces
17	clothes, dresses, Inuit
19	Canada, Mexico City
20	geyser, minutes, pyramid, waterfall, Wyoming
21	Arizona, canyon, Washington, D.C.